KNITHOARD

Claire Crowther

HAPPENSTANCE

ACKNOWLEDGMENTS:

Thanks are due to the editors of the online journal *The Clearing*, in which two sections of this sequence first appeared.

To Jen Arnall-Culliford and Frome Stitch 'n Bitch for technical support, encouragement and laughs—many thanks.

Gratitude also to Stockwell poets (Anne Berkeley, Sue Rose, Siriol Troup, Tamar Yoseloff) and Helyar poets (Fiona Benson, Patrick Brandon, Julia Copus, Jane Draycott, Carrie Etter, Annie Freud and Jenny Lewis) for responding to early drafts of these poems.

BY THE SAME AUTHOR:

BOOKS:

Stretch of Closures (Shearsman, 2007)
The Clockwork Gift (Shearsman, 2009)
On Narrowness (Shearsman, 2015)

PAMPHLETS:

The Glass Harmonica (Flarestack, 2003)
Incense (Flarestack, 2010)
Mollicle (Nine Arches, 2010)
Silents (Hercules Editions, 2015)
Bare George (Shearsman, 2016)

Printed by The Dolphin Press
www.dolphinpress.co.uk

First published in 2019 by HappenStance Press,
21 Hatton Green, Glenrothes, Fife KY7 4SD
nell@happenstancepress.com
www.happenstancepress.com

CONTENTS

KNITHOARD: A GLOSSARY OF TERMS

block—method of shaping knitted pieces before making up

dec—knitting instruction: 'decrease'

ease—the difference between the measurement of a knitter and her garment

Fair Isle—a technique of colour-knitting originating in the Shetland Islands

fingering—a thin three- or four-stranded yarn

gauge—a measure of tension

hap—a knitted cape

laceweight—a thin, two-stranded yarn

nalbinding—an ancient form of knitting

notion—any item of knitting equipment

peerie—tiny, applied to a stitch in a Fair Isle pattern

ply—a measurement of the number of strands in a yarn

PSSO—knitting instruction: 'pass slipped stitch over'

purl—a stitch made by knitting into the front of a stitch

round—a row of knitting that returns to its beginning

stash—a knitter's hoard of wool

steek—a piece of knitting that has been cut

swatch—a sample piece knitted to measure tension

tension—the tightness or looseness of stitches

For Mary Henderson,
the Fair Isle designer who enlightened me

'Re-clothe us in our rightful mind'

—John Greenleaf Whittier

THE PAPER PATTERN

I was laid under the lilac
not much made ...

I was laid under the lilac
being born in May.
All the pattern was in my body.

I opened my eyes to rough leaves
blowing apart and broken.

Now I can hold a leaflet
of shape with a picture and how to make it,
I can read the pattern on paper
and try to make

and every evening lay it down
not much made ...

LEARNING THE PATTERN

My terms are hard.
Pearl.

My terms are hard.
Cast.
Cast off.

I've misheard
harsh sounds.
PSSO.
Steek.

I've misread
words.

Purl?
Pearl?

PATTERN FOR FOUR NEEDLES

My project was to be
a fourth needle.

My project was to be
socks that week.

A hole of stitches grew
from a stretcher of endless
needles. And which needle
sealed that sole, that heel?
The first, the second, the third?
The turn

of each round made its trinity
while I knitted on
a fourth needle.

CIRCULAR KNITTING

Not such a weird carry on
through yarn's universe.

Not such a weird carry on?
Four double pointed pins? Angels, a googleplex.

And what is called round, though it comes round,
feels straight and how could there be purl there
where I knit—no purl, all knit—
yes, I knit, I knit but I didn't do purl

yet when I turned the flue of stocking stitch
inside out,
a sea of purl purled on in there.
I watched its waves tunnel
through yarn's universe.

HANDMADE

I am quick but I have to be perfect
to be paid.

I am quick but I have to be perfect.
Not one mistake
though mistakes are proofmarks of makers.

My heart-side needle is fixed.
The right-side needle flashes knives.

My knuckles are hard as stone and swollen.

I've been long enough in the practice to hate the work.
I've scored each peerie stitch on my fingers.
Every strand of this yarn
binds me to do what I have to do
to be paid.

A FIT OF DIFFERENCE

None of these patterns calls for
my whole stash.

None of these patterns calls for
my body

nor do my measurements match
the superficial categories:
man, woman, child

though every pattern summons
a body to rise
from the yarn bowl. Shape comes
in flocks. Clothe me in one hap,

I'll give up
my whole stash.

TENSION

My tension
fully matches the gauge.

My tension
denies the knitprint, the swatch
that proves I knit out of true
as an outfit should never be knitted.

I am instructed over and over:
Change your yarn,
use bigger notions.

When I won't switch needles,
I screw up the pattern.
But no swatch
fully matches the gauge.

AUCTION

Will I win the wool?
Is it my time?

I will win the wool,
bidding tonight on Ebay.

At the final moment of auction
I'll bind all bidders off.

I'll wind my bargain in
while lower offers fall away like people

who will tender again for yarns from elsewhere—
the Falklands   India   Japan

cones and skeins
messed with and rewound.

Now, in my bed jacket, at nearly closure,
is it my time?

Claire Crowther

THE DROP

When the slippery needle slides out of its row
what a vacant sort of vision that is.

When the slippery needle slides out of its row
and falls silently
down from whosever precipice of lap
it lies on:
its stitches quiver and peer
out from behind each other,
each empty
O
an eye
newly opened.

What a vacant sort of vision that is.

THE DROP (2)

Once it has been blindly
pulled up again ...

Once it has been blindly
put in a mass
swathe of stitches bound
to each as each is being
bound

the circle pulls

out of itself through oval to undone.

Still, it could be tweaked
back over the bar
of the row below

pulled up again ...

THE DROP (3)

The dropped stitch
will be discarded.

The dropped stitch
might shoot thanklessly
through a finished fabric

while the steel bolt
which must deliver
every last stitch into clothing

does not know, I think,
what even the stitch knows

that all coats
will be discarded.

CHARITY

Aren't they everywhere, the lost?
Will I bring them home?

Aren't they everywhere, the lost?
Dead sweaters. Abject vests.
The forwardness of their stitchery
admits: *We are handmade,*
we have been held and put down.

Each one is hung, packed tight,
a stitch in a row.

That blue cabled Donegal cardigan.
That worsted hap.
Will I buy them?
Will I bring them home?

THE AUTOCRATIC JACKET

Although I narrowed the ease of it,
in the end I gave it away.

Although I narrowed the ease of it
to my tight tension

although I started by hoping it would grow
to fit my arms, only mine,
loose enough for my sore neck

although I knitted its bodily parts together
and the beads of pattern touched only my fingers

after a while I, even I the owner,
could not hold its intricacies in my lone imagination.

Because it held itself off

in the end I gave it away.

SHORN

line after line is broken
but I am heard

line after line   is broken
off I stitch
again and again   shorn

row
upon
row
I write   for you

cut, myself, I cut   for you
you
shear the stuff from my mind
but I am heard

FLY STRIKE

Sheep share. They don't steal
maggots from their own backsides.

Sheep share. They don't steal.
Their hair hangs in handfuls
from hedges and barbed wire fences.
I gather the thin and plentiful wisps.
This is their yarn. They have to shed it.
How hot they must have been,
Bluefaced Leicester, Gritstone,
to accuse me: *You hair-free humans*
who haven't shorn us,
you have turned away from us,
maggots from our own backsides.

HAIR AND HUBRIS

My own cover, mine, my fine hide, my
mantle of hair ...

My own cover, mine, my fine hide, my
paws itch to stitch
strands of my flesh

to comb my bones
to laceweight

to make filaments
of my veins.

But I can't work
my own blanketing—

thin, too thin, my
mantle of hair.

FLOCK

I want the inheritance
of shared hair.

I want the inheritance
of practicalities.
The knitting machine has to punch its cards,
its electromagnets must cling on.

Yet I have to name belief as well as work it.
Which family title identifies
the hairiness of beings?

Me, a Shorthaired Part-fleeced Hobs Moat?
You, a Thickhaired Whole-fleeced Shetland?
We are the family *Sheep*
of Shared Hair.

OLD LOVERS' PARADOX

No thread through age though sleep is
bound to increase.

No thread through age though sleep is.
Night spools in to the Minotaur and out.
I must wake up and I have to wake alone.

But daytime is joint
and the weave is agreed
so each day I cast on and increase.

Yet, where two are
knit together,
the pattern says *Dec.*

You're not, it says,
bound to increase.

A WINTER VIEW OF THE NESS

I will finish abandoned garments, cast off all
my Fair Isle.

I will finished abandoned garments, cast off all
those vests sleeping in bags and drawers,
all the unfinished

bands and edgings half dissolved,
half hard as the clinging snow
that lies in fingers along
our neighbouring ness.

I'll rest the last fractals of Shetland.
The snow will shrink its own
patterns to show
my fair isle.

THE WARM WORK IS DONE

I'll cast off all think
at the row's end.

I've cast off all think

of cold, knitting together
so many couplets of stitches.

My nalbound love,
our rows were rosaries.

Two bamboo needles
graced our bed.

Their brown grain plied on
and on till there was no

warm thread to hold
at the row's end.

PRAYER TO THE WOMAN CLOTHED
WITH THE SUN

I've worn
my singularity.

I've worn
your hair.

Woman of the sun, unwind it now.
Lady of shine, shake out your rays.

I pray:
unlace me from my stitchery.

If I must block this hap,
cowl knitted for comfort

the cloth that shoulders
the hell of being borne

help
my singularity.